Beautiful
New York®

"Learn about America in a beautiful way."

Beautiful
New York®

Concept and Design: Robert D. Shangle
Text: Craig Ryan

First Printing November, 1980
Revised Edition
Published by Beautiful America Publishing Company
P.O. Box 608, Beaverton, Oregon 97075
Robert D. Shangle, Publisher

Library of Congress Cataloging in Publication Data
Beautiful New York
1. New York, N.Y.—Description—Views. I. Ryan, Craig, 1953—
Library of Congress Card Catalog 79-90287
ISBN 0-89802-003-4
ISBN 0-89802-004-2 (Hardbound)

Photo Credits

GENE AHRENS—*page 19; page 22; page 30; page 43; page 47; page 48; page 52.*

MARGARET ANNALA—*page 35.*

ED COOPER—*page 17; page 20; page 21; pages 24-25; page 26; page 27; page 29; page 31; page 32; page 33; page 34; page 36; page 37; page 38; page 39; page 42; pages 44-45; page 46; page 49; page 50; page 51; page 53; page 54; page 55; pages 56-57; page 58; page 59; page 60; page 61; page 62; page 63; page 64.*

JOE DIMAGGIO, JOANNE KALISH—*page 23.*

MICHAEL MELFORD—*page 28; pages 40-41.*

BOB MEYER—*page 18.*

**Color Separations
by
Universal Color Corporation
Beaverton, Oregon/San Diego, California**

Contents

Enlarged Prints

Most of the photography in this book is available as photographic
enlargements. Send self-addressed, stamped envelope for information.
For a complete product catalog, send $1.00.
Beautiful America Publishing Company
P.O. Box 608
Beaverton, Oregon 97075

Introduction

There's no telling who first called it the Empire State, but the name fits. "Empire" suggests a land that's lordly, far-reaching, all-encompassing—and there you have New York. From the crowded canyons of Wall Street to the summit of Mt. Marcy a mile in the sky, the state is dense with superlatives. It's a list-maker's dream: the long line of illustrious residents, the numerous historical traditions, the cultures, the industries, the arts—and most of all, the inexhaustible array of natural beauty. But New York is much more than a catalog of firsts, bests, tallests, and mosts. There is a great synthesis of wilderness and human energy here that sets the state apart and distinguishes it in the eyes of the world.

The first men probably came into New York by way of the Niagara Peninsula: descendants of Asiatic nomads who crossed the Bering Strait into North America eventually found their way here. These early men were primarily roving hunters and fishermen. Much later the Algonquin Indians managed to establish the first agricultural communities, and it was the Algonquins who were there to greet the European ships that began to appear in the harbors. It was about this time that the Iroquois started moving into the area. With their genius for political organization, they were able to displace the Algonquins and gain control of what would one day become New York State. Originally, the Five Nations of the Iroquois battled the French explorers, befriending the Dutch and English. But before long the great Iroquois confederacy split, and by the time the American Revolution had ended, the Indian dynasty, sadly, lay in shambles.

Samuel de Champlain, a Frenchman, and Henry Hudson, in Dutch employ, headed the earliest expeditions into the interiors of New York. They arrived at approximately the same time in 1609, beginning a struggle for control that would last 150 years. Dutch fur traders erected some of the first permanent settlements near what would become the state capital. By 1760, Dutch, English, and Scots populated the frontier settlements, but New York still ranked only seventh in population among the 13 colonies.

New York played a crucial role in the War of Independence. Almost one-third of the Revolution's battles occurred on New York soil. And after the fighting was over, the settlements began to expand. Suddenly, with both the British and the Indians no longer a threat, the colonists were able to turn their hands to building a nation. They cleared trails through the forests and built their cabins on the far frontiers. But New York City, at the beginning of the 19th century, had nowhere near the commercial prominence it enjoys today. That took the digging of the Erie Canal and the steady stream of goods that flowed along its path. The city flourished. By 1850 the state ranked number one in industry and commerce, and near the top in agriculture. And with its rapidly increasing population, it was fast becoming the pre-eminent political force in the nation. During the Civil War, the canals declined in importance while the railroads and factories proliferated. Industrial capitalism had come to New York for good, and the dominant base that would carry the state into the 20th century was realized: specialized agriculture, manufacturing and commerce.

The special flavor of a place and its people is contained best, perhaps, in its folklore. And there's no shortage of that in New York. The mountainous regions of the state are rich in yarns and legends. James Fenimore Cooper and Henry Wadsworth Longfellow both appropriated Indian lore for their tales, which remain integral parts of New York—and American—historical consciousness. Washington Irving, who knew the legends of the Dutch, populated the hills with the likes of Rip Van Winkle and the Headless Horseman. Tales abound among the Hudson Valley folk of ghosts who search for buried gold by moonlight beneath the waters of Annsville Creek, and at Tappan Zee you'll hear of goblins and witches. Legends abound concerning Captain Kidd and his buried treasure, and to this day New Yorkers search for the fortune off Gardiners Island and dig for it along the banks of the Hudson. There are those who will swear the footsteps of Kidd's murdered bride can still be heard, pacing in front of the house in which she waited for him to return. There are tales of Old Meg the Hag, a tall, withered mountain woman with yellow skin and a three-inch beard who possessed supernatural healing powers; and of a slave ''witch-finder'' named Tashee who traveled the countryside with an arsenal of talismans and amulets, casting spells on the tombs of dead witches so that they might never again rise from their slumbers. There are likewise a healthy number of ballads and salty worksongs that have been passed down through the generations. The winters in the Adirondack lumber camps were hard, and the men sang songs just to forget the cold; and some fine folksongs come from the days of the Erie Canal.

The folklore, the landscape, the history, the culture—New York is rich. And this wealth of elements produces an atmosphere, a special personality that sums up New York.

C.R.

Land Beyond the City

From across the East River, the great monoliths of Manhattan loom. On certain mornings they appear poised like dinosaurs frozen to a steamy slab and at night they light the sky like fireworks. The city is awesome, riveting, omnipotent. Even in Central Park, surrounded by the sweet green of grass and trees, the skyscrapers rear above to throw their reflections in the duck ponds. When it all builds up to a weariness that might be called metropolitan exhaustion, the city dweller must go somewhere to search out the peaceful quiet of the land.

While much of the rest of the country, familiar with New York only through television, may imagine that the city spreads so far and so fast that one would need to board an airplane to outrun it, the New Yorker knows that in an afternoon he can get to pristine ski slopes, hike in a 30,000-acre forest, or kick sand on a barren stretch of beach. There are two directions to go: east onto the forked tail of Long Island, or north along the Hudson River Valley. In both choices are limitless recreational possibilities and a chance to soothe the soul in the unchanging visage of nature.

The crooked finger of Long Island extends 120 miles to the east and north from Manhattan. There are roughly seven million people on its 1,723 square miles, but the farther you go, the fewer people you'll see. Out on the very tip of South Fork are stretches as deserted as the moon. When you cross one of the bridges into Brooklyn or Queens, you're on ''The Island.'' Traditionally, it has been a playground of the very rich: J.P. Morgan, F.W. Woolworth and William Vanderbilt all made their homes here. Teddy Roosevelt's mansion still stands. There are 14 state parks and miles and miles of beach. The Long Island Sound is off the northern shore and the Atlantic Ocean off the southern. The Island is famous for its oysters and ducks (Long Island Duck appears on menus coast to coast). And surprisingly, Suffolk County is the leading county in the state in terms of agricultural dollars, mainly in potatoes.

But the natural beauties of the Island are found on the far peninsulas and on the elongated barrier beaches off the south shore. North Fork, once the center of the oyster industry, and still raising some of the finest oysters anywhere, is a true sports paradise. Watersports and fishing are popular, as are golf, bird watching, and horse-back riding. And out on Orient Point, you feel as if you were on Cape Cod. The village is provincial New England-ish and the coast is strangely mysterious.

Between the forks, in the Block Island Sound, is privately owned Gardiners Island, granted to the Gardiner family by the King of England three centuries ago. Rumor has it that the buried treasure of Captain Kidd is hidden here. Certain areas on South Fork (like East Hampton and Hampton Bays) are fashionable vacation colonies, but others retain a flavor of the old days. Sag Harbor was a major whaling port in the 19th century and still hangs on to the trappings of the whale-boats and sailing ships. And out on the Montauk Peninsula is true wilderness. There are thousands and thousands of acres of wooded countryside, cliffs and gullies, coastline, sand dunes and even fresh-water lakes that serve as temporary homes to flocks of migratory swans. The air and water are quite unspoiled here, and the beaches and dunes rank with the finest in the nation. The fishing is excellent as well. Venture into the deep Atlantic for swordfish, tuna or marlin, or keep your feet on dry land and cast into the surf: your chances are good.

The barrier beaches off the south coast of the Island are popular with New York-ers. Jones Beach, the largest state park on the Atlantic Coast, is about 2,500 acres of woodlands and sand. Fire Island is a 40-mile strip of sand dunes and beach adminis-tered by the National Park Service. There are no roads at all on this island, but 25,000 people line it each summer.

The Hudson River is something of a paradox. Its valley north of the city is a magnificent counterpart to the Rhineland in Germany. Cliffs and forested mountain ridges stretch into the hazy distance from its banks. Yet its primary function is as a tool of commerce and industry without which New York City might never have existed, much less prospered. And the service of the city has threatened the river's health. The Hudson, therefore, has become a source of controversy. Environmental-ists point to the disappearance of the shad and the fact that the Hudson's waters are no longer safe for drinking or swimming. The industrialists claim that the pollution has not affected the physical glories of the river valley: the waters still sparkle and surrounding woodlands remain hypnotically captivating. Whatever your point of view, the Hudson Valley is lovely today, there's no denying that. State parks along its shores offer lake swimming, boating, camping and hiking. And the splendor is aug-mented by the deep historical traditions of the area. George Washington slept here, Franklin Roosevelt lived there, British and American troops fought Revolutionary War battles over there, and right down the middle of it chugged Fulton's steamboat. The list is almost endless.

East of the river, out on Long Island Sound, is Ward Pound Ridge Arboretum, some 50 miles of stunning trails, and in winter there's skiing, sleighing, and tobogganing. Fishkill is a popular recreation center and at Clarence Fahnestock State Park, the bass and trout are plentiful. A little farther north is Taconic State Park along the Massachusetts border (camping, fishing and skiing are all good) and beyond, Catamount Ski Area on the edge of the Berkshire Mountain region. Nearby, in Kinderhook, is the setting for Washington Irving's *Legend of Sleepy Hollow*, a fact celebrated in the local communities.

West of the Hudson is Sterling Forest Gardens, a skiing area surrounded by thousands of acres of heavy forest and a gigantic, well-managed garden with elaborate fountains and exotic birdlife. And Manhattan is only an hour's drive away.

The Catskills

A guidebook's gloss might offer something like this about the Catskills: "A popular and easily accessible mountain park less than 100 miles north of New York City, a favorite vacation spot famous for its luxurious resorts and physical charm." Indeed, for a good part of the 20th century the American mind imagined the Catskills as primarily a group of swank hotels where Lower East Siders went to honeymoon, drink, socialize, and, most of all, be entertained. The woodlands were but a handsome backdrop.

This steep country west of the Hudson began to become fashionable decades ago as the white clapboard inns and houses of Sullivan County gradually gave way to stucco-and-timber Swiss chalets and ultimately the massive fortresses of the big hotels like Grossingers'. Pretensions to elegance came tramping to the woods and soon transformed any existing notions about the place into a tourist cliche: Capital of the Borscht Belt.

But attitudes began changing sometime in the 1950s, and the area blossomed, revealing its true splendor. This is a splendor that existed long before the posh resorts, a lushness not only of wilderness and wildlife, but of history and legend, hermits and visionaries, ghosts and artists. The resorts, with their self-contained "vacation environments," have far from disappeared. In fact, they continue to thrive. But the Catskills today are celebrated in a simpler style, and the urban weekender, venturing toward the high ground, is more apt to be decked out with khakis, sleeping bag and fishing tackle than the latest in leisure-wear and pool fashions, infinitely better prepared to snatch a glimpse of the Catskills' undeniable magic.

One funny thing about "the Mountains" (as these rugged forestlands are known): they're not really mountains at all. A geologist will tell you that the cliff-crowned swells of the Catskills are simply a part of the Allegheny Plateau (which stretches from Tennessee to Canada) that stuck up high enough to be sliced into crags and crevices by the forces of wind and water. The tallest peak along this dissected ridge is barely over 4,000 feet and there are just a few natural lakes. But regardless of what you call them, they are an amalgam of timber-lined rock faces, shaded streams, dense ravines, and sunny green valleys; a garden of gnarled pines and polished boulders, blooming with huckleberry, rhododendron and mountain laurel.

Everything but the enchantment seems nebulous in the Catskills, even the name. "Catskill" would make a challenging subject for even the expert toponymologist (one who studies place names). As late as the 18th century the area was being called Kaaterskill by some of the Dutch, and the Blue Mountains by the British. "Kill" seems certainly to come from the Dutch word for stream or inlet. But scholars have suggested also that the name derives from Indian words, from wildcats (literally, "cat's kill") and, oddly enough, the Flemish word for the game of tennis. Confused? That's business as usual when dealing with the Catskills.

Even the boundary lines around the Catskill Mountains make for a tricky subject. People have argued about it for a couple of centuries and they're not through yet. One old-timer, living near the edge of the Catskills, was asked where they began. "You keep on going until you get to where there's two stones to every dirt," he replied, "then, you're there." An approximate definition would place the Hudson River on the east and the Delaware River on the west, and would include the area from Stamford south to Bethel. On the whole, it has a haunting, sleepy charm.

Mist hangs from these hilltops on summer mornings and rises gracefully from the cool streams full of trout. One especially popular trout stream is the Esopus, which is dammed at one point, creating the huge Ashokan Reservoir. The Ashokan and other manmade lakes have brought new recreational possibilities to the Catskills, and fishing them will usually yield a respectable catch of bass and pickerel. The weekend camper won't see a variety of big game, but he should see lots of deer: they're everywhere in the Catskills. There are some bear, too, but this is mainly a place for the small critters like fox, mink, raccoon and porcupine; also game birds such as pheasants and grouse. And once you've been there, when you've poked around a little, climbed the peaks, fished the cool streams, and sat to watch the sun disappear and the forest grow dark and still, you forget the geologist and nod off to sleep. No doubt about it, these are the mountains.

If you talk to any long-time Catskill residents you're likely to hear about the Patent sooner or later. It's a long story of border disputes and legal maneuvering that still carries bitter overtones. In 1708 Queen Anne of England granted a million and a half acres of land (encompassing nearly all of the Catskills) to Johannis Hardenbergh and seven other men. This became known as the Hardenbergh Patent. Ostensibly, the grant was made to reward Hardenbergh for bravery in the War of Spanish Succession, though it is now believed that Hardenbergh was in the Catskills for the duration of that war and that the Great Patent (as it is also known) amounted to nothing less than a monumental land swindle. It would take volumes to unravel the events surrounding the patent, but suffice it to say that settlers were upset, learning that they were suddenly tenants on someone else's property. Predictably, the whole business of the patent touched off a series of disputes that may never be resolved, and with the disputes came the inevitable reprisals.

But greed for land and money is hardly the only thing the Catskills have inspired in the men and women who settled here. Since the beginning, these glens and brooks have attracted the artist and free-thinker. Some of the first world-renowned stories to come out of America had their origin in the Catskills. Washington Irving brought the region to life for readers everywhere, and painters and engravers have also found the mountains and village scenes a rich subject matter for centuries. The American romantic Thomas Cole, in particular, succumbed to the spell of the Catskills. His canvases shimmer with the rich meadows, wind-swept ridge-tops and eerie haze settling in the green-black gorges. Unique folk arts (woodcraft especially) can be seen in the isolated hollows. Architecture here comes in styles of an unbelievable variety: from the rough-hewn lean-tos and country cabins to improbable palaces that suggest ancient Greece or the resplendent castles of Bavaria.

Woodstock, Byrdcliffe and Maverick were all thriving art colonies in the early days of this century. The Catskills have always lured the dreamers, those who believed that a life in the woods under the hypnotic hand of nature somehow authenticated an existence that would remain forever mundane in the cities. The bowling balls of Rip Van Winkle might still be heard echoing through the hollow hills, they claimed, for those with imagination. And they came in droves: students of painting, music and dance, communes where alternative lifestyles were tried, and a long list of festivals that celebrated serenity and chosen brotherhood. There were problems at first when the older mountain folks were faced with the influx of such unconventional types. One can imagine the incredulity with which an old mountaineer gawked as two dozen toga-clad dancers came skipping over a rise with wildflowers in their hair and the melodies of Mozart trilling from their lips. As the colonies grew more settled, tourists began trooping into the mountains just to verify the outrageous tales they had heard of mad Bolshevik poets and sun-worshipping nudists. They weren't often disappointed.

The past few decades have seen a network of good roads built through the Catskills. It might be argued that such construction is an insult to the natural grace of the area. However, these roads have been instrumental in making the Catskills available to man in ways never conceived before. They probably have a great deal to do with the new attitude toward the mountains. In fact, a good method of exploring the

Catskills is to head in by car, being sure to leave the road map at home, and let your instincts navigate. It won't take long to find the areas and activities that interest you. Hiking may be the surest method of finding the wilderness, and the extensive trails here are well-marked and furnished with lean-tos for rainy nights. The less-daring summer sportsman will find golf courses and even a race track at Monticello Raceway to supplement the fine fishing. In winter there is tobogganing, sleighing, skating, and a gamut of ski and snowmobile areas.

One last note: although the Catskills (as part of the State Forest Preserve) are protected by law, threats to their continued health come from all sides. The romance of the wild attracts more and more backpackers and nature-lovers each year. Most will have a good sense of the ecological balance and tread softly, yet the inevitable souvenirs of the city find their way here in increasing quantity. Soil erosion along the trails is also becoming a problem. Commercial recreation facilities share the blame: mountain slopes have been dynamited in order to improve the skiing. The suggestion has been made that new efforts to protect the Catskills are in order. Perhaps the public outcry that saved the Adirondacks in the 19th century might now be directed toward these lazy hills to insure that generations to come will have a chance to know their be-witching beauty.

Upstate:
The Adirondacks
and the
Thousand Islands

A short drive from the State Capital at Albany puts you suddenly in the mountain wilderness of the Adirondacks. The resorts and tourist hang-outs are there; if that's what you're looking for. But if you forsake the state highways for some peculiar-looking gravel road and take off on foot, you'll find wilderness as remote and unspoiled as you have ever dreamed of. Perhaps you'll stumble onto a trout stream hidden in the forest, shaded by spruce and hemlock, or a cool mountain lake that no one else seems to have discovered. Spots like these still exist in the Adirondacks.

Unless you're familiar with the geography of the state, you'd be amazed at just how much of New York is made up of the Adirondack Park. It is truly immense, its 8,900 square miles making it larger than the state of Massachusetts, and bigger by far than any national park. Nearly two-and-a-half-million acres of it are state-owned wilderness, which means it "shall be forever kept as wild forest land."

The Adirondack Mountains are the oldest in the world. Once taller than the Rockies, time has worn them down and mellowed their character, though their majesty remains intact. Mt. Marcy is the summit, standing at 5,344 feet. And while it is often assumed that the Adirondacks are a part of the Appalachian chain, they are in fact a separate range.

Until the 1830s the granite masses of the Adirondacks remained relatively unexplored and were not even named until 1837. But timber operations moved in quickly and began clearing the land until Franklin B. Hough discovered what was happening. Hough was conducting the state census in 1865 when he became aware of the systematic denuding of the mountainlands. (As a result of these logging practices,

Autumn color in the Adirondacks

Mt. Colden and Mt. Marcy from Algonquin Peak

Mt. Marcy

Ausable Chasm

New York City skyline
(Following pages) Fort Ticonderoga from Mt. Defiance

Winter scene in the Catskills

23

Farm country near Dryden

Hudson River near Mechanicville

St. Lawrence River at Moses State Park

Adirondack State Park

29

Lake Champlain Bridge, Crown Point

Spring water in the Catskills

Skaneateles Lake, one of the Finger Lakes

Lake Placid, Whiteface Mountain

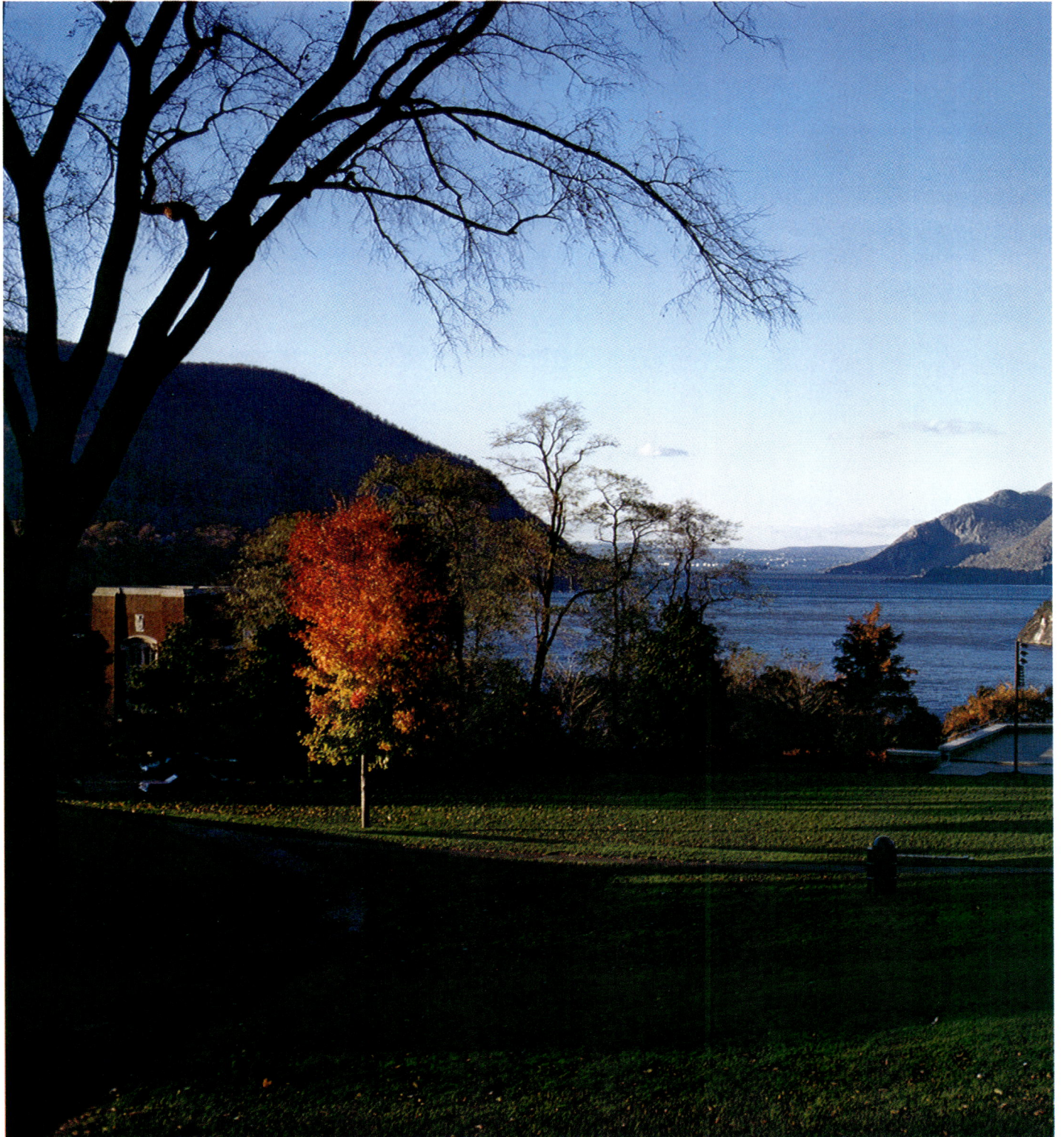

View of the Hudson River from West Point

Horseshoe Falls—The Canadian Niagara

Lake Ontario from Lake Bluff

Lake Placid from Whiteface Mountain

Fort Ticonderoga

Whiteface Mountain, Adirondacks
(Following pages) Evening in New York City

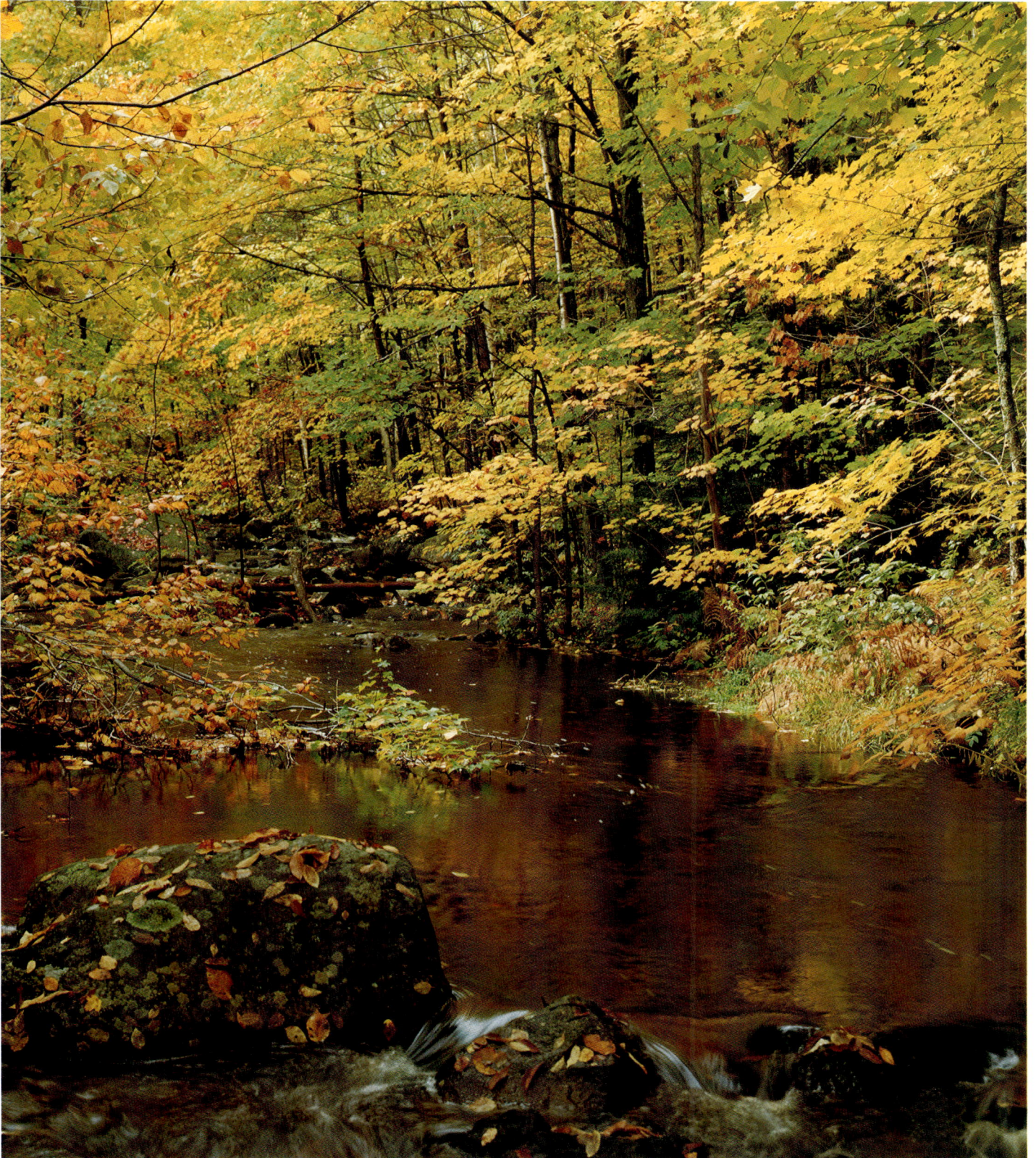

Brook near Port Henry
(Following pages) Tupper Lake, Adirondack State Park

Mohunk House, Mohunk Lake

43

Bear Mountain Bridge, Hudson River

Stream in the Adirondacks

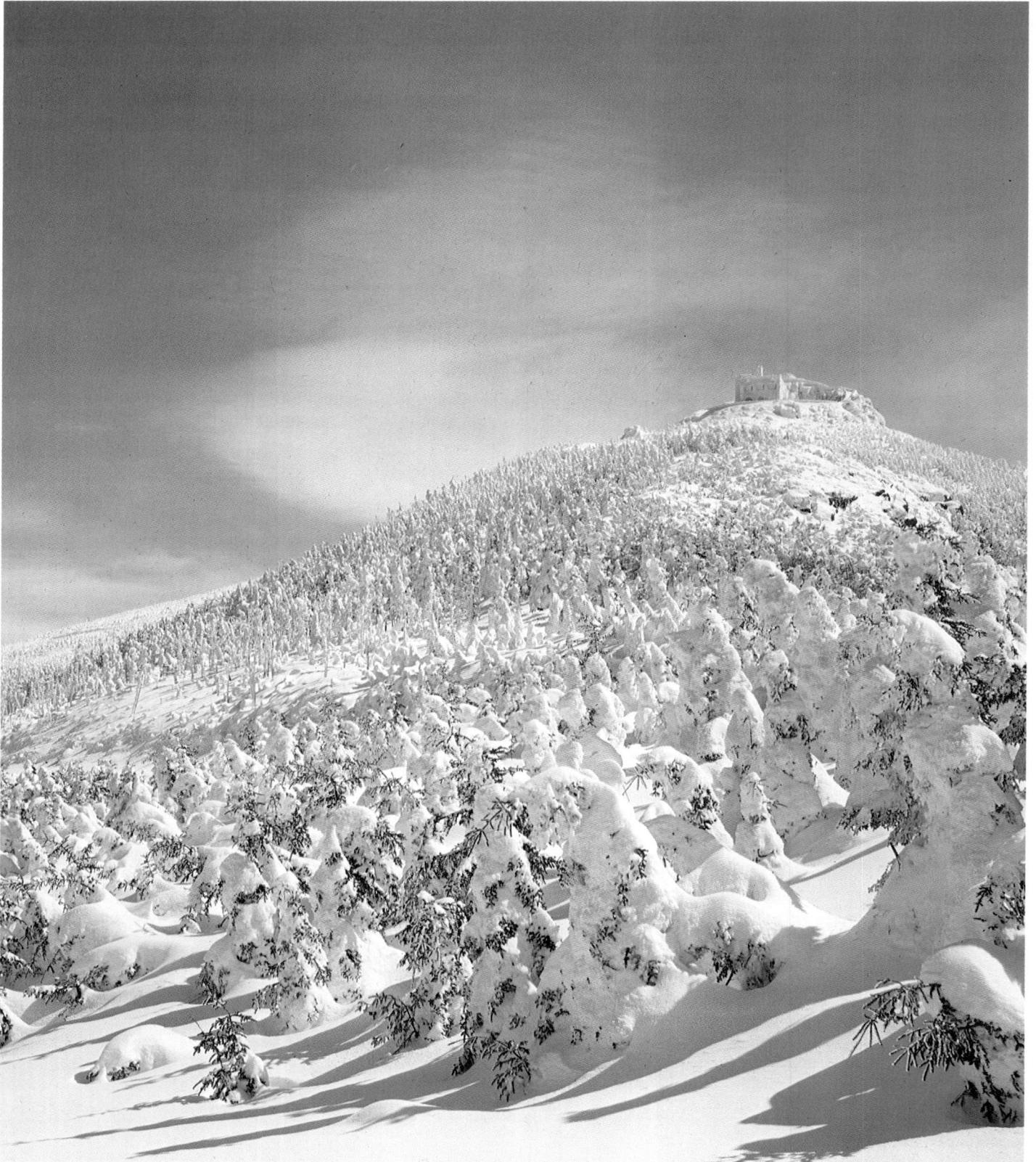

Whiteface Mountain

Bunchberry, slopes of Mt. Marcy

New Paltz and farmlands from the Shawagunk Mountains

Sunrise on Lake Erie

View from Stone Tower, Allegheny State Park

Raquette River

53

Genesee River Gorge, Letchworth State Park
(Following pages) New York City skyline from Staten Island

Watkins Glen State Park

Middle Genesee Falls, Letchworth State Park

Meadow near Oneonta

Seneca Lake

Lilies, golden grain near Stone Mills

Lake Ontario from Lake Bluff

Buttermilk Falls

most of the timber seen here today is second and third growth.) He influenced state legislation to halt the ravages of the timber concerns. The Adirondacks' next hero was Verplanck Colvin, a lawyer and engineer, who supervised measures that led to permanent protection of the area from profiteers. Colvin (who has since had an Adirondack Peak named for him) climbed Mt. March in 1872 and discovered the source of the Hudson River and Lake Tear-in-the-Clouds. As a temporal reference, it's interesting to note that explorers of the Pacific Northwest had discovered the source of the Columbia River 60 years earlier!

There are an impressive number of lakes in the Adirondacks (some small and unknown, others spectacular and famous) and uncounted streams stocked with trout, bass, perch and—surprisingly—some salmon. One-hundred-fifty species of birds have been identified, and, in addition to the deer and black bear, creatures like fox, rabbit, coyote, beaver, raccoon and porcupine abound. The granite boulders are nestled with white pine, black spruce, hemlock, balsam fir, mountain ash and maple. And if all this is not enough to send the urbanite packing to the hills, the mean temperature is always 10 degrees cooler than New York City, quite an attraction given the sweltering Gotham summers. There are 500 miles of hiking trails and unlimited skiing opportunities for those still unconvinced. And should the notion that thousands of others will get the same idea and follow you into the mountains give you pause, remember that the Adirondack Park is big enough for just about everyone and that total isolation is always available if you're willing to travel the unbeaten path and seek out those obscure spots not written up in any brochure or guidebook.

The lakes are worth special mention. Champlain and George are the major ones, both long fingers of water in the eastern Adirondacks near the Vermont border. Both attract a great many tourists. Lake George, with its commercial recreation attractions and blue waters full of boats and perhaps a seaplane or two, contains over 100 islands, some of which are available for camping. And Lake Champlain offers some extraordinary views of the Green Mountains in Vermont. It's little wonder Champlain and George are so popular. But lakes are scattered all through the mountains, many inaccessible by road and a few completely remote. Sometimes they're called ponds: Moose Pond and Raven Pond are two. There is also Lake Placid, surrounded by some of the highest peaks in the Adirondacks and one of the finest spots for winter sports.

It would require considerably more space than is available here to get specific about the Adirondacks. The park is so overwhelmingly vast, and there are so many fascinating pockets, each with its particular attraction and beauty, that it seems impossible to begin. The best places to find the true wilderness, of course, are those unknown to most people—and the less said about them, the better. If you've got the desire, you'll find your own private space anyway. But there is a spectrum of local

Canadaway Creek, south of Dunkirk

65

color throughout the park and each nook seems to shine with its own hue. The people who settled this region and gave it human substance may not be more interesting than those elsewhere, but they certainly seem to be. Racquette Lake and Dannemora serve as examples of the historical and cultural color.

Racquette Lake lies about 15 miles west of the town of Blue Mountain Lake in the central Aidrondacks. It's part of the Fulton chain of lakes thta link up to provide a 150-mile canoe route from Old Forge to Loon Lake. Racquette is the largest of the chain and is easily accessible from State Highway 28. There is a vintage resort on the southwestern tip from which boat trips are launched. The lodge building more or less defines the typical Adirondack lodge: a peculiar combination of elements of the Swiss chalet and the log cabin. This is one of the best hunting and fishing areas in the Adirondacks and wildlife is plentiful. Alvah Dunning, celebrated in local legend as the finest of the 19th-century guides, killed his first moose here at age 11. Supposedly, Dunning also bagged the last moose to fall in these mountains, sometime before the Civil War. Dunning is notorious for his antisocial behavior and defiance of urban man's codes. He described the casual woodsmen who began drifting up to the mountains as ''city dudes with velvet suits and pop guns, that can't hit a deer when they see it, and don't want it if they do hit it.''

Dannemora is a town in the northeastern Adirondacks, particularly mountain-ous terrain, named for the Swedish city: the connection is that both have iron deposits of exceedingly high quality. The history of the region is tied up with mines and the labor of the miners. Convicts were imported from the cities to work the rugged mountain lodes. These workers quickly learned how cold and harsh Adirondack winters can be and dubbed the place ''Siberia of the North.'' Offenders are still housed at Clinton State Prison, but the iron mines have been supplanted by farming and various light industries. State Highway 374 creeps around the shoulder of Dannemora Mountain west of town and descends to Chazy Lake on the other side. From the lake is a scenic hiking trail to the summit of formidable Lyon Mountain. Lyon is also known for the quality of its iron deposits: the massive cables of the Golden Gate Bridge in San Francisco derive their strength from these slopes. A few miles to the north is Lower Chateaugay Lake, and the route of the highway guides the sightseer through a spectacularly primitive wilderness. Here is a hint of the sort of country where one might find that much sought-after isolation.

Other notable spots in the Adirondacks, if somewhat less eccentric, include Ausable Chasm, a one-and-a-half-mile gorge several hundred feet deep cut by the Ausable River. It contains a series of waterfalls, rapids, and eroded rock formations of spectacular proportions. Whiteface Mountain near Wilmington, one of the Adirondacks' tallest and most awesome peaks, accessible by an eight-mile road that goes nearly to the summit (there's a trail to the very top), boasts 28 separate ski slopes. Another by-product of the powerful Ausable River is High Falls Gorge, where a chain of waterfalls plummets 700 feet and is surrounded by some of the most intense foliage and wildflowers found anywhere.

While not part of the Adirondack Park, the Thousand Islands on the St. Lawrence River lie just to the north. Actually the islands number about 1,700, and since the St. Lawrence forms part of the border between New York and Ontario, some of them belong to Canada. Certain of the islands are nothing more than rocky points that nose above the water level, sprouting a scrawny dwarfish tree, but others are spacious enough to accommodate whole villages and glorious mansions. Gazing on some of the larger ones, it's difficult to keep fantasy at bay: the ornate castle-like fortresses push proudly from thickets of trees, surrounded on all sides by the peaceful waters. Surely everyone has dreamed of having an island to himself.

To the Iroquois Indians, the Thousand Islands area was known as Manitonna (Garden of the Great Spirit). To them it was the epitome of the happy hunting ground of their legends. It was an early French explorer who dubbed them the Thousand Islands, though his estimate (probably intended as an exaggeration) came up short. Names of the individual islands provide descriptions of their own: Needle's Eye, Lost Channel and Devil's Oven. Many of them have been designated state parks.

A scattering of colorful towns along the river share in the region's special aura. Clayton, for instance, sits on a peninsula jutting out into the St. Lawrence: it's a fishing and vacation center with a crowded schedule of dances and concerts during the summer months. The St. Lawrence freezes over each winter, so most folks visit the area between June and late October.

Fishing is a rewarding activity on the St. Lawrence and the best spots are between Cape Vincent and Ogdensburg. Each year anglers haul plenty of bass, pike, pickerel, muskellunge and trout from the waters. The other big recreation attractions are swimming and canoeing. Guided boat tours are also popular and a variety of yachts leave Alexandria Bay (resort center of the Thousand Islands) daily. To the south is International Bridge, linking the U.S. with Canada via several of the islands.

Central and Western New York

The area we call central and western New York makes up nearly half the state, running in a wide swath from the Adirondacks toward the Great Lakes. The diversity of the region has caused it to become known as something of a microcosm of America: agriculture produces everything from wine grapes and fine cheeses to onions and carrots; a variety of industries manufacture a boggling array of products; there are beaches, lakes, mountains and wide plains, an Indian reservation, wildlife preserves and several large, cosmopolitan cities. The region consists of three main sections: the large chunk of land in east-central New York that runs from the Catskills and the Mohawk Valley toSyracuse and Binghamton; the beautiful Finger Lakes country; and from far western New York out to Niagara Falls and up north to the Canadian border.

The region's amazing productivity can be traced to the early years of the 19th century and the pet project of Governor DeWitt Clinton. He wanted the world's longest ditch dug clear across the state, from Buffalo to Albany. They called it Clinton's Folly and it took 15 years to accomplish, but the project was the Erie Canal. This was the single most important engineering effort in the history of the state. Suddenly you could ship a ton of wheat from Lake Erie to Albany on the Hudson for just ten dollars. Before the canal, the shipping charge would have been about $100.

The benefits were immediate, and towns became cities all along the route. A real folklore sprang up around the canal, and especially its workers. The boatmen who rode the great barges the breadth of the state were a colorful bunch, boozers and notorious gamblers to a man. But this is all nostalgia today. The era of the great canal has passed along with infamous Side Cut section of West Troy (a neighborhood of nothing but bars) where the boatmen gathered to blow off steam. A fair amount of traffic still uses the Erie Canal, but the Chenango System from Syracuse to Binghamton is no longer in use. Technological advances allowed the building of a superior waterway, the New York State Barge Canal, which continues to deliver goods and haul products for the cities along its path.

One part of New York that benefited from the Erie Canal is the Mohawk Valley, in the east-central part of the state. Utica, once a textile center, is the principal city. Today its economy is diversified with a variety of industries, including a trio of high-quality breweries. Along the Mohawk River is the town of Herkimer, a major cheese producer, and to the south is the Russian Orthodox community of Jordanville. Monks who left Russia at the time of the revolution established a monastery and seminary here, and the flavor of the place remains exotic. Farther west along the canal route is Oneida, site of a well-known silverware factory and, in the 19th century, John Noyes' experimental utopian community. A few miles away in Canastota are some of the finest architectural mementos of the Erie Canal's heyday.

The Finger Lakes region of central New York epitomizes the natural beauties of the state. According to Indian legend, the long, narrow lakes were created by the fingers of the Great Spirit, stroking the land. There are six large lakes (Canadaigua, Keuka, Seneca, Cayuga, Owasco and Skaneateles) and five smaller ones. Besides the lakes there are deep gorges, streams and rolling fields. The land is fertile and, hence, the Finger Lakes region is an agricultural center. And as New Yorkers know, it's a popular vacation spot, with more than 20 state parks.

On the western edge of the Finger Lakes is perhaps the most spectacular spot of all. Fifty miles south of Rochester, the Genesee River runs through Letchworth State Park where it has carved a massive gorge 600 feet deep and 17 miles long. The scenic Gorge of the Genesee has been dubbed the ''Grand Canyon of the East,'' and wild rapids and waterfalls tumble along its entire length.

Another particularly spectacular attraction of this region is Watkins Glen. There is a famous auto race here and it is one of the major salt producing spots in the country, but the state park steals the show. There is another magnificent gorge here, along with a network of dark grottos, trails and waterfalls. During Labor Day weekend in 1934, a reporter spotted a deer stranded on an inaccessible ledge high above the gorge. The story hit the papers and the next day more than a quarter of a million New Yorkers showed up to view the spectacle, many of them trying for days to lure the confused animal to safety. A series of ingenious measures, including the building of a bridgeway across the gorge, all failed. Then, one night, the deer somehow managed to scramble down the precipice and escape to safety. At Watkins Glen are some striking waterfalls. Montour and Pluto Falls are two of the major ones, and Chequaga Falls are illuminated for visitors on summer nights.

The highest waterfall east of the Rockies is at Taughannock Falls State Park near

Trumanburg. Set in a scenic gorge, its waters spill 215 feet. This is the Cayuga Lake region where a rich farm area at Cortland becomes a vacationland each winter. Montezuma National Wildlife Refuge is here, also, dedicated to the preservation of wildfowl. And for scenic beauties, the quiet town of Skaneateles must be experienced. The lake here has been called ''the most beautiful body of water in the world,'' and not without justification. There is a relaxed quaintness to the area, reflected in the series of country lanes winding away from the lake and into the green landscape.

South of Geneva, in the area between Canandaigua and Keuka Lakes is the New York wine country. Oenologists worldwide have praised the fine wines of the lake country. Naples and Hammondsport are two of the principal wine towns, and winery tours are available at several locations. Though grapes are the key to the area, lots of potatoes are grown here and the world's biggest buckwheat mill is in Cohocton. And the foliage in fall must be seen to be believed.

South of the Finger Lakes, near Elmira and the Pennsylvania border, is the sailplane capital of the nation. The wide, table-top plain called Big Flats sits in the center of a natural bowl formed by the Chemung Mountains, and gliders continually fill the air. A bit farther west is Allegheny County, one of the few places left where wild turkey are plentiful (so much so that the big game birds can be hunted—in season, of course). Nearby is Olean, site of the early New York oil fields, where remnants of a prehistoric sea and a huge natural quartz display can be seen.

Next door is the enormous Allegheny State Park, 57,000 acres of wooded highlands on a bend of the Allegheny River. There is an extensive network of mountain streams and miles of hiking trails. The shores of Lake Erie are not far away and the countryside here is known as the Southwest Gateway. The Lake Erie Plain covers much of it: hilly forestlands of hardwoods that turn the colors of fire each autumn, miles of vineyards and fruit orchards and a couple of lakes. The Chautauqua Country is to the north and fishermen have hauled muskellunge in excess of 40 pounds from Chautauqua Lake.

By far the most celebrated of natural wonders in the state of New York lies at the extreme western edge: Niagara Falls. Sacred to the Indians, who heard the thundering voices of their gods in the cascading foam, the series of falls drop water 326 feet between Lake Erie and Lake Ontario. The first European to see the falls was a French missionary who visited them in 1678. The falls endured a long period of commercial exploitation before coming under the joint ownership of New York State and the Province of Ontario, Canada. This became New York's first state park. The Niagara River (technically an inland strait), covers a distance of 36 miles between the Great Lakes. And as the water gushes over the rocks and gradually polishes them down, the falls move upstream—about one foot per year. Estimates have them backed up all the way to Buffalo in about 130,000 years.

Niagara Falls actually consists of three main waterfalls: American Falls (the highest), Canadian—or Horseshoe—Falls (the widest), and Bridal Veil Falls. It's a good idea to try and see them from a number of vantage points because their characters change radically as you move about. The best view of all three fall crests is at Prospect Point. The 70-acre Goat Island in the middle of the river offers a good close-up view. There are a number of scenic auto routes, boat trips and even helicopter rides, and Niagara Falls should be seen at night for the most romantic visage. There are some good state parks along the river, too, especially Devil's Hole and Whirlpool, where recreation and splendid forest foliage abound.

Beautiful America Publishing Company

The nation's foremost publisher of quality color photography

Current Books

Alaska	Maryland	Oregon Vol. II
Arizona	Massachusetts	Oregon Coast
Boston	Michigan	Oregon Country
British Columbia	Michigan Vol. II	Pacific Coast
California	Minnesota	Pennsylvania
California Vol. II	Missouri	Pittsburgh
California Coast	Montana	San Diego
California Desert	Montana Vol. II	San Francisco
California Missions	Monterey Peninsula	San Juan Islands
California Mountains	Mormon	Seattle
Chicago	Mt. Hood (Oregon)	Tennessee
Colorado	Nevada	Texas
Dallas	New Jersey	Utah
Delaware	New Mexico	Utah Country
Denver	New York	Vancouver U.SA.
Florida	New York City	Vermont
Georgia	Northern California	Virginia
Hawaii	Northern California Vol. II	Volcano Mt. St. Helens
Idaho	North Carolina	Washington
Illinois	North Idaho	Washington Vol. II
Indiana	Ohio	Washington, D.C.
Kentucky	Oklahoma	Wisconsin
Las Vegas	Orange County	Wyoming
Los Angeles, 200 Years	Oregon	Yosemite National Park

Forthcoming Books

Alabama	Kauai	Oahu
Arkansas	Maine	Phoenix
Baltimore	Maui	Rhode Island
Connecticut	Mississippi	Rocky Mountains
Detroit	New England	South Carolina
The Great Lakes	New Hampshire	South Dakota
Houston	North Dakota	West Virginia
Kansas		

Large Format, Hardbound Books

Beautiful America	Beauty of Washington	Volcanoes of the West
Beauty of California	Glory of Nature's Form	Western Impressions
Beauty of Oregon	Lewis & Clark Country	